Our Global Community

Music

Lisa Easterling

Heinemann Library
Chicago, Illinois

Customer Service 888-454-2279
Visit our website at www.heinemannraintree.com

Designed by Joanna Hinton-Malivoire
Photo research by Ruth Smith
Printed and bound in China by South China Printing Co. Ltd.

11 10 09 08 07
10 9 8 7 6 5 4 3 2 1

The Library of Congress has cataloged the first edition of this book as follows:
Easterling, Lisa.
  Music / Lisa Easterling.
     p. cm. -- (Our global community)
  Summary: This text introduces readers to different kinds of music and the role it plays in society.
  Includes bibliographical references and index.
  ISBN-13: 978-1-4034-9406-1 (hc)
  ISBN-13: 978-1-4034-9415-3 (pb)
  1. Music--Social aspects--Juvenile literature. [1. Music--Social aspects.] I. Title.
  ML3928.E27 2007
  780--dc22
                          2006034297

Acknowledgements
The publishers would like to thank the following for permission to reproduce photographs: Alamy pp. **15** (Mauricio-José
Schwarz), **16** (AAD Worldwide Travel Images); Corbis pp. **4** (Tim Pannell), **6** (Gideon Mendel), **7** (Jim Zuckerman), **9**
(Richard T. Nowitz), **10** (M.A.Pushpa Kumara/epa), **11** (Gavriel Jecan), **14** (Free Agents Limited), **17** (Royalty Free), **19**
(Bruce Connolly), **20** (Bob Sacha), **21** (Lindsay Hebberd); Eyewire pp. **22** (musical instrument images); Getty Images pp. **5**
(National Geographic), **8** (Stone), **12** (Robert Harding World Imagery), **13** (Blend Images), **18** (Photonica).

Cover photograph reproduced with permission of Getty Images/Imagebank. Back cover photograph reproduced with
permission of Getty Images/Blend Images.

Every effort has been made to contact copyright holders of any material reproduced in this book. Any omissions will be rectified
in subsequent printings if notice is given to the publishers.

The paper used to print this books comes from sustainable resources.

Contents

Making Music

People make music.

People make music in many ways.

People make music by clapping
their hands.

People make music by stomping their feet.

People sing.

People play instruments.

How People Play Instruments

People play instruments with their hands.

People play drums with their hands.

People play instruments with their fingers.

People play guitar with their fingers.

People play bagpipes with their mouths and fingers.

People play flute with their mouths and fingers.

People play music together.

People play music alone.

Why People Play Music

People play music to celebrate.

People play music on special days.

People play music to dance.

People play music for fun.

Musical Instruments

String Instruments

Wind Instruments

Percussion Instruments

Picture Glossary

celebrate to show that you are happy about something

instrument something that you play to make music

Index

Note to Parents and Teachers
This series expands children's horizons beyond their neighborhoods to show that communities around the world share similar features and rituals of daily life. The text has been chosen with the advice of a literacy expert to ensure that beginners can read the books independently or with moderate support. Stunning photographs visually support the text while engaging students with the material.

You can support children's nonfiction literacy skills by helping students use the table of contents, headings, picture glossary, and index.

2/11.